Musings & More

GUNJAN SHAH

First Published in February 2019

ISBN: 978-93-5347-191-0

BLUE ROSE PUBLISHERS

www.bluerosepublishers.com

info@bluerosepublishers.com

+91 8882 898 898

Cover Design:

Mohit Joshi

Typographic Design:

Sonia Suyal

Distributed by: Blue Rose, Amazon, Flipkart, Shopclues

Acknowledgements

Compiling my poems and drafting them as a book is harder than I thought and more rewarding than I could have ever imagined. None of this would have been ever possible without my parents, Mrs. Madhu Shah and Mr. Paresh Shah, they are the reason behind all this taking the face of reality. If it wouldn't have been them pushing me to put my best foot forward and also letting me follow my passion without any pressure, supporting me in all the decisions of my life.

I'm eternally grateful to acknowledge my elder brother Mr. Eshaan Paresh Shah, as it is literally impossible to imagine all this happening without his support, he is like the 'Steve Jobs' behind my own iteration of 'Steve Wozniak', and also getting my work known to the world.

Art needs inspirations and inspirations are nothing but experiences. So, I would like to acknowledge all the people, things, memorable instances, and everything that has inspired me to put forth my efforts. Thanks to all those who have been an integral part of my getting here. My friends for constantly going through all my work and suggesting me all the most suitable changes that could enhance it even more. I would like to Thank Bhavya Parekh, Tej Khandor, Nirmit Gosar and Kajol Mehta for supporting me from very beginning of my journey, and constantly being eager to read my poems. I would like to acknowledge Riddhi Veera and Sreehari Menon for brainstorming and helping me zero down to a good title for the book. Thanks to Harshil Padada and Jay Vira for constantly suggesting me newer ideas to work upon. I would like to thank Ayush Pillai for helping me put the cover page as a sketch, and Mr. Wilford Machado, to take time out of his busy schedule and carry out a photoshoot for the Cover page of the Book. A special thanks to Harshita Sharma and Chetan Nayak for editing my work.

Finally, I would also like to mention Blue Rose Publishers and the entire team for putting forth the best effort along with me, coping up with all my requirements and issues, helping me out at every step of publishing, it would have been impossible without them.

THANK YOU EVERYONE
FOR MAKING MY DREAM COME TRUE!!

एक क्षण में, न जाने क्या हो जाएगा,
किसे पता है के आखिर, प्रलय कब आएगा?

प्रलय!

एक क्षण में, न जाने क्या हो जाएगा,
किसे पता है के आखिर, प्रलय कब आएगा?
ना तू किसी को परास्त कर, उसपर फतह पाएगा,
इसीलिए जीवन का आनंद ले, ए बंदेया!
क्योंकि मृत्यु आने पर, सब यहीं धरा रह जाएगा!!

एक क्षण में, न जाने क्या हो जाएगा,
किसे पता है के आखिर, प्रलय कब आएगा?
अंत में ये शरीर अस्थियों में मिल जाएगा,
इसीलिए जीवन का आनंद ले, ए बंदेया!
क्योंकि मृत्यु आने पर, सब यहीं धरा रह जाएगा!!

एक क्षण में, न जाने क्या हो जाएगा,
किसे पता है के आखिर, प्रलय कब आएगा?
अपने किए हर करम का फल तू ज़रूर पाएगा,
इसीलिए जीवन का आनंद ले, ए बंदेया!
क्योंकि मृत्यु आने पर, सब यहीं धरा रह जाएगा!!

I'll Be There for You!

Until sometime ago, we weren't even acquaintances,
Between us there were a lot of distances,
Us talking to each other were very rare instances,
Maybe it was due to the barrier of the religious differences

Since the time I know you, I have known the true
meaning of love,
If your hands feel cold and shiver, I'll be the glove,
Seeing you happy is the Goal of my life,
And I'll always be with you till I am alive.

In a world where true love seems to be lost,
I'll love you always, no matter what the cost.

You've been there for me, and I vow I'll be there too,
I have always wanted the company of someone like you,
If you're sad, I'll crack jokes, old as well as new,
I just want you to know, I'll be there for you!

The Open-Eyed Nightmare!

This day feels like an open-eyed Nightmare!
With monster eyes, does the Demon stare!
All the excitement disappears in thin air,
Being a part of this is the worst "I Swear!"

Shit happens in front of your eyes, which you can't tolerate,
But the only option you've got is to wait,
No matter how hard you try, you can't outwit your fate,
Thus, it's better you realize, before it's too late.

You try to forget it and just be calm,
But shit just keeps happening like the un-snoozable alarm,
You didn't want this to happen, and do you any harm,
And wish someone would help you, and hold your arm!

You wish someone was with you, someone did care,
But all you can find is a sky full of despair,
With monster eyes, does the demon stare!
This day feels like an open-eyed nightmare!

The Girl I Love Always Loves Someone Else!

Every time that I have fallen for someone,
And I think that she is the one.
Something inside me holds me back,
And I too feel that I ain't on the right track!

Due to the past experiences I get afraid,
All those memories never tend to fade.
I keep loving someone, just to find out,
That there is someone else, whom she wants to ask out!

This feeling inside me gets very deep,
Restless and Crazy, I am unable to sleep.
I don't know what all to tell you, and what not to say,
Coz I know that you're destined to leave me and walk away!

Why do I have to always make way, for someone else?
Why does the girl I love, always love someone else!

I Didn't Know It Was Bound to End This Way!

I knew it, that this would happen someday,
All of a sudden, we might start drifting away,
And to each other, there will be nothing left to say,
But I didn't think it would end this way!

It's all due to this ungrateful day,
That the bond we had, began to decay,
I was hoping that forever it would stay,
And it wasn't meant to end this way!

Maybe now it's not worth the delay,
Blaming each other was how we used to play,
And whatever good we had we did give away,
But I didn't know it would end this way!

"What you deserve will come to you" is what they say,
I didn't know it was bound to end this way!

To Love I Lost A Friend!

I don't know why, this time, things didn't mend,
Slowly with time, maybe this was to end.
I ain't sad, but I think it's unfair,
For this sudden let down, you gave me no time to prepare.

Every memory ran down like a flashback,
But I had to burn it all along with the Haystack!
I don't know what was going on in your mind,
Or was it me, who in love was completely blind!

Knowing we weren't going to get along,
I still decided to give you everything I had,
You were completely mean to me,
And treated me in a way terrible and bad!

I just wanted to have someone with whom I could relate,
But now you're a person whom I truly hate!
For you though I was sleepy, I used to stay awake,
Maybe falling in love with you was my mistake?!

It ended quicker than it began,
I wish it had lasted for a longer time span,
When you didn't feel the way I did, why did you pretend?
Because of you, to love I lost a friend!

A Poetic Affair!

During my school days this thing happened,
I felt affectionate towards a girl pretty and cute,
For me, she was the definition of inner and outer beauty,
The feeling pumped me up, and the story had just begun.

It took no time, and I fell for her,
That face flashed suddenly and would also
suddenly disappear.
Thinking of her, I used to go insane,
I used to stroll in the vicinity, following her lane to lane.

I described her beauty and started writing rhymes,
Though I couldn't express it to her, even on valentines.
Soon after that, we had to undergo counselling,
As all my actions, for her, weren't at all appealing.

Though the Girl I fell for, didn't feel the same for me,
Every moment that I spent thinking of her,
is a now a pleasant memory.
After all the ups and downs, we both are still friends,
Though we both are living our lives leading us
to different ends.

It doesn't matter whether she chose to get along, or my
proposal she did reject,
It was her decision, and for those words
I have immense respect.
She still looks cute with the same smile
and the short hair,
It was nothing but a sweet little Poetic Affair!

Take Me Back to The Night We Met!

Take me back to the night we met,
When there was nothing between, not even regret,
All that remains now is disgust and disrespect,
Take me back to the night we met.

All the memories, now I am trying to forget,
Now I hate someone that not long ago I used to respect,
It's too late now, and those feelings won't resurrect,
Take me back to the night we met.

What was the reason that the dots didn't connect?
Was it my mistake, was I too direct?
Or, was is something completely different,
some unknown aspect?
I need to know the reason as to why is
everything wrecked,
Take me back to the night we met!

Though Always with Me,
You Actually Were Never There!

The feelings that we had, are to be found nowhere,
Maybe this thing on both sides is unjust and unfair,
All that remains is nostalgia along with the nightmare,
Though always with me, you actually were never there!

Some of the best moments of life with you I did share,
I miss teasing you, and pulling your long hair,
Despite everything that has happened, I still do care,
Though always with me, you actually were never there!

The way you played your part,
do you think it was fair?
You should also question yourself,
to find the answer hidden somewhere,
It can't be my fault every time, everywhere!
Though always with me, you actually were never there!

Confidant

It takes no time to get used to someone,
When they are around, you are all pumped up
and having fun,
They are the reason for a smile on your face,
In your life they fill in a special place.

They are there for you all day long,
Supporting you every time, no matter you are
right or wrong,
Every place you go, they always tag along,
They motivate you and make you feel strong.

A moment without them, and you start to feel miserable,
Once again to the weaknesses you are vulnerable.
Every moment, every place becomes Nostalgia,
As it is them who help you through each
and every Phobia.

All they think about is your prosperity and your welfare,
True friendship is very rare and beyond compare!

अकसर

अकसर में यह सोचता रहा कि कौन है वो
जो मेरे ख्वाबों पर सवार है,
जाने क्यों लगता है हमारे बीच एक धुंधली सी दीवार है,
मुझे लगता नहीं मेरा मन उस राज़ को जानने को तैयार है,
परंतु उस दीवार को भेदने के लिए मन बेकरार है।

शायद उस परछाई को भी मेरी तलाश है,
लेकिन किसी कारणवश वो मुझसे नाराज़ हैं,
या उसके भेद को जानने के मेरे प्रयास से वो निराश है,
मुझे उकसाने का शायद उसका ये कोई प्रयास है।

ना जा!

ना जा, मुझे छोड़ के, यूं मुझसे दूर,
इतना तो बता दे, क्या था मेरा कसूर।
क्यों करती है तू ये बार बार,
क्या यही मेरी गलती थी,
के मैंने किया था तुझसे प्यार!!

ना जा, देकर मुझे आंसू, करके आंखें नम,
थी तू ही इबादत मेरी, तुझमें ही था धरम।
छोड़ कर जब जाती है, हो जाता हूं बेचैन और बेकरार,
क्या यही मेरी गलती थी,
के मैंने किया था तुझसे प्यार!!

ना जा, मेरी जान, तुझमें बसी है मेरी धड़कन,
करम का पलटेगा जब पासा, दिखला देगा वो तुझे दर्पण।
तेरे और सिर्फ तेरे लिए, छोड़ने चला था में घर संसार,
क्या यही मेरी गलती थी,
के मैंने किया था तुझसे प्यार!!

मुझको फिर से हो गया है प्यार!!

सुन रे सुन, ओ मेरे यार,
मुझको फिर से हो गया है प्यार!
ख्वाबों में मेरे आती है वो बार बार,
मुझको फिर से हो गया है प्यार!!

खूबसूरत इतनी, मानो हो कोई अप्सरा,
उसकी आवाज़ का दीवाना हो गया है, दिल ये मेरा।
सोच रहा हूं, के कर ही दूं इज़हार,
मुझको फिर से हो गया है प्यार!!

है ज़हन में मेरे उसी की धुन सवार,
देख नैनों को उसके, अपना दिल मैं गया हार,
उसके आगमन से छा जाता है खुशियों का त्यौहार,
मुझको फिर से हो गया है प्यार!!

यही करता हूं मैं, जब होता हूं बेकार,
इसीलिए तो दोस्तों,
मुझको फिर से हो गया है प्यार!!

Between Us

Everything that I had for you, is now covered in dust,
Everything disappeared with the arrival of the gust,
You were the one, I thought I could blindly trust,
But all that is left between us, is only disgust!

There was a time, when for everything,
we used to take the same route,
I was unaware of the fact,
that it was only you in the picture throughout,
Now it is all clear, in my mind there is no doubt,
Maybe this is why, from everything that's happening
around, I want an out!

All the memories of us together, I will compile
and then combust,
In the current scenario there's no chance that
I can adjust,
You do all of your mind,
even after it is all mutually discussed,
Now, it doesn't matter,
whether it was just or unjust,

There is nothing you can do now,
to regain my trust,
As all that is left between us,
is only disgust!

All I Do Is Rant!

Irrespective of what it is, all I do is rant,
Even If at some distant place, it's just a holy chant,
Or it is some dirty jeans, or some worn out pant,
Irrespective of what it is, all I do is rant!

Irrespective of what it is, all I do is rant,
When the lunch comprises of something I dislike;
like eggplant,
I never give it a thought, whether can I do it or I can't'?
Irrespective of what it is, all I do is rant!

Irrespective of what it is, all I do is rant,
When the line is straight and even when the line is slant,
Maybe I'll do it even when I undergo
some organ transplant,
Irrespective of what it is, all I do is rant!

Irrespective of what it is, all I do is rant,
Even when it's enough, and even when it is scant,
And even while watching basketball alongside
Kevin Durant,
Irrespective of what it is, all I do is rant!

In My Mind!

I don’t know why,
though I left everything about you behind,
You are still there, you are still in my mind,
There have been countless instances,
sitting all by myself, I have whined,
But you are still there, you are still in my mind!

Towards you and your memories my heart
is still inclined,
You are still there, you are still in my mind,
Thinking of you all the time,
I am emotionally confined,
You are still there, you are still in my mind.

Something about you,
still makes me feel you are one of a kind,
Maybe that’s why, you are still there,
and you are still in my mind.
Someone like you, I will never be able to find,
You are still there, you are still in my mind!

Hey! Quit Playing Games with Me!

There have been countless instances,
when I have told this to you,
But every time, you just act weird,
as if you don't have any clue.
If you don't have it in you,
to take it all seriously, Then,
Hey! Quit playing games with me!

I am tired of all this, and don't want
to start a blame-game,
Because whatever I have to say,
you counter it with reasons pretty lame.
If you don't feel the spark, then go away,
and also set me free,
And please, quit playing games with me!

Just admit it, being with me,
did nothing but only brought you shame,
I won't mind you going away,
ven without you it will be just the same.
I guess it's my fault, it's not my cup of Tea,
Maybe I should stop fooling around,
and playing games with thee!

I know, it is only my half and not the entire story,
If you vow to leave me, I'll never cross paths,
or enter your territory.
It will never be back to how it all used to be,
So, Hey! Quit playing games with me!

तबाही

ना जाने ये कैसा दौर आया है,
नहीं कोई अपना, ना कोई पराया है,
चंद लम्हों में मैंने सब कुछ गवाया है,
ऐसी स्थिति में सबने खुदको विवश पाया है,
सिकंदर भी कहां अपनी तबाही से बच पाया है!

जीवन का सार इस क्षण में समाया है,
तू है तो इंसान ही, चाहे खुदको कीर्तिमान बनाया है,
तेरा हर करम, तुझे लेकर यहीं पर आया है,
ऐसी स्थिति में सबने खुदको विवश पाया है,
सिकंदर भी कहां अपनी तबाही से बच पाया है!

तैयार हो जा नादान, कठिन समय निकट आया है,
तेरा अंत संग चल रहा, मानो तेरा साया है,
चंद क्षण शेष रह गए, अपना पूरा जीवन कर दिया तूने ज़ाया है,
इस स्थिति में, तूने खुद को अकेला पाया है,
याद रख, सिकंदर भी कहां अपनी तबाही से बच पाया है!

संग होकर भी तू मेरे संग नहीं !

चला था जिस राह से,
आ खड़ा हूं मैं फिर वहीं,
सोचा था मैंने के,
खुशी मुलाकात होगी मेरी कहीं !

तेरे संग संग चलने के,
ख्वाब मैंने देखे थे कई,
सोचा था तुझ संग,
बनाऊंगा हसीन यादें नई !

तेरे होने का एहसास जैसे,
करता कोई जादू था,
तेरी बातों में खो गया,
हो गया मैं बेकाबू था !

करता रहता था खुद से ही,
मैं अकसर तेरी बातें,
ख्वाहिश थी यही के,
तेरे संग ही बीते सारी रातें !

कहना ज़रूर चाहता था,
तुमसे हो गई है मुझे मुहब्बत,
पर कोई और ही वजह थी,
जिससे थी तुम्हारे चेहरे पर मुस्कुराहट!

करनी थी बातें कई,
रह गई जो अनकही,
तुझपर दिल लूटा दिया, और जाना,
संग होकर भी तू मेरे संग नहीं!

Time to Bid You Adieu!

Even before its outbreak, it is time to bid you Adieu,
A lot was going on inside, that I couldn't tell you,
Within such a short span of time,
I had starting falling for you,
And I am well aware, that you didn't even have a clue!

I still remember that day, when I first met you,
I felt fresh, as if it was the beginning of something new,
Just exchanging looks, not concerned about
the rest of the queue,
I felt something special, unsure whether
you felt the same way too!

To know how I felt, you would have
to step into my shoe,
But you were already dreaming yourself with someone
that had always been with you,
You were in your happy place, and I didn't want to
screw it all for you,
I still will always be there,
as I see a very good friend in you!

A lot was going on inside, that I will never tell you,
Even before its outbreak, it is time to bid you Adieu!

I write this because...

I write this, because when you left,
You left nothing but pain!
I write this, because you are the reason,
I hide my tears, in the pouring rain!

I write this, because all your memories,
Still drive me insane!
I write this, hoping that from now on,
We never face each other again!

I write this, so that there's nothing left in between,
Which can be a reason to complain!
I write this, because even after putting efforts,
The equation was hard to maintain!

I write this, because being with you,
I felt like a person held captive by a chain!
I write this, to remind myself that,
I was addicted to you, as someone to cocaine!

I write this, because when you left,
You left nothing but pain!
I write this, because you are the reason,
I hide my tears, in the pouring rain!

Why?

Even after putting the best foot forward,
Why is it that, my efforts don't bear me any fruit?
Even though I am not at fault,
Why I am always asked to stay mute?

Even after trying so hard,
Why do I always find myself,
in some or the other dispute?
Even after taking everything into account,
Why do I always miss something very minute?

Even after putting forth the best I can,
Why don't I receive any applause or a salute?
Instead of doing things in the right manner,
Why do I always end up choosing the wrong route?

Even after putting the best foot forward,
Why is it that, my efforts don't bear me any fruit?
Even though I am not at fault,
Why I am always asked to stay mute?

www.ingramcontent.com/pod-product-compliance
Ingram Content Group UK Ltd.
Pitfield, Milton Keynes, MK11 3LW, UK
UKHW040014200726
13854UKWH00001B/195

9 789353 471910